CASSANDRA COMPLEX

Claire Cooper
of New Walk Museum
Leicester
Sent me this (July 2018)
as a gift from
Jonathan Taylor
the author of this book.
It was my condition
for my granting him
permission to use
'Messiah' by Ernest Neuschul
as the cover of this book.
Khalil
10th July 2018

CASSANDRA COMPLEX

JONATHAN TAYLOR

A collection of poems, found poems, found translations,
mis-translations, prophecies, pseudo-prophecies, apocalyptic
visions and moments of retroactive clairvoyance.

Shoestring Press

Printed by imprintdigital
Upton Pyne, Exeter
www.digital.imprint.co.uk

Typesetting and cover design by narrator
www.narrator.me.uk
info@narrator.me.uk
033 022 300 39

Published by Shoestring Press
19 Devonshire Avenue, Beeston, Nottingham, NG9 1BS
(0115) 925 1827
www.shoestringpress.co.uk

First published 2018
© Copyright: Jonathan Taylor
© Copyright cover image: Ernst Neuschul, 'Messias' (1919), image supplied courtesy of the Artist's Estate and Leicester Arts & Museums Service

The moral right of the author has been asserted.

ISBN 978-1-912524-17-4

ACKNOWLEDGEMENTS

Thanks to Nick Everett, Corinne Fowler, Scott Freer, Jo Walton, Harry Whitehead. Special thanks to John Lucas. Thanks and love to my mother, my family, and, of course, Maria Taylor. Earlier versions of these poems previously appeared in the following anthologies, magazines and webzines: *Allegro Poetry*, *Clear Poetry*, *Edgar and Lenore Journal*, *Ekphrastic Review*, *Envoi Magazine*, *Eunoia Review*, *Firefly Magazine*, *Fulcrum*, *The Gull Magazine*, *I Am Not A Silent Poet*, *Ink, Sweat & Tears*, *Interpreter's House Magazine*, *Knot Literary Magazine*, *Lakeview International Journal of Literature and the Arts*, *Letter Press Project*, *Levure littéraire*, *The Lonely Crowd*, *Monster Anthology*, *The Morning Star*, *Ofi Press*, *Peeking Cat Poetry*, *Please Hear What I'm Not Saying*, *Plume Magazine*, *Poetic Diversity*, *Poetry Scotland*, *Prole Magazine*, *Rialto Magazine*, *Silver Birch Press*, *Strands*, *The Stare's Nest*, *Strike Up the Band*. Many thanks to all the editors involved. Thanks too to the University of Leicester and Authors for Grenfell.

Dedicated with love to Miranda and Rosalind

We are on a perilous margin when we begin to look passively at our future selves.

— George Eliot, *Middlemarch*

CONTENTS

1st MVT

LIAR

Long before presidents seemed so crazy
(though that might well have been illusory),
long before anyone mentioned global warming,
before wars were anything but bottled messages
washed up on the sinking island of childhood
and before disease bludgeoned you to death
over godforsaken months and years,
I cracked my head open on a metal railing.
In hospital you held my hand when I cried
and told me everything—head, world,
et cetera—would be okay. You lied.

TELEOLOGY I

It is no very good symptom either of nations or individuals that
they deal much in vaticination.
– Thomas Carlyle

You might catch a glimpse of toga
like a slip beneath the manager's
pressed suit, doctor's white coat,
economist's titillating bar-charts

for the prophets are everywhere
spouting a cacophony of futures
on screens, stages, street corners
in Medieval Latin, Ancient Greek.

There is a wind-up Nostradamus
in your head. Just for tonight
let him wind down, shut curtains
on Cassandras crowding like triffids,

like refugees from an Apocalypse
yet to happen, and do something
future-less.

TELEOLOGY II

The refugees from an Apocalypse yet to happen
are flooding through the time-gate in bloodied rags,

marked by the Antichrist, trembling from earthquakes,
scorched by stars and planets crashing to earth,
chewed and spat out by dragons with various heads,
nibbled by locusts.

Tens of thousands have already perished en route
and most who reach their past are denied sanctuary:
after all, it's their fault they weren't among the Elect.
The future can hardly be blamed on *us*, can it?

A select few we save, those who bring with them
knowledge of soon-to-be-discovered technologies,
oh, and the plumbers.

The others—the godless, hairdressers, authors—
are shoved back,
whingeing they can't win on either side of history.

Afterwards, if you press your ear against the door
and listen carefully, I have heard it said,
you can hear trumpets, distantly, from the other side.

BEDTIME AT 9

so George Bailey was never born, wouldn't hear
Clarence get his wings, lost Zuzu's petals forever.

Roger Thornhill was stuck as George Kaplan
& crop-dusters dusted no-crops on & on.

Sister Maria never came back from her convent
to kiss & marry Plummer, climb every mountain

& this might've turned me into a pessimist
but at least history was frozen sometime late '30s,
Österreich never quite reaching *Anschluss*.

Only music creeping upstairs into dreams
afforded an ambiguous form of prolepsis,
fortune-telling in muffled songs, marches.

CRAB SUPERNOVA, AD 1054

Free translation from the account by Ibn Butlan

When the pestilential guest star appeared in Gemini
the cemeteries of Constantinople overflowed:
14,000 were buried in St. Luke's alone.
Midsummer, it spread to Egypt when the Nile was low
and the dead outnumbered the stars in Old Cairo
taking with them all foreigners of the city except those
whom Allah willed to live. Here in Iraq, as Saturn
descended into the sign of Cancer, warring factions
were decimated by a pestilential truce, a treaty
drawn up by plague. In Mosul, Jazira, Diyar Bakr,
Rabica, Mudar, Fars, Kirman, lands of the Maghrib,
Yemen, Fostat and Syria, the story was the same:
first black-bile ulcers all over the body, the spleen
swelling up, fevers and agonies, death.
Thus when Saturn and Mars were in conjunction
in the sign of Cancer Ptolemy's wise prediction
for the East was confirmed: that infection
of the skies by a guest star would spread to Earth,
that a star's *influence* would become *influenza*,
and famine, plague, strife, sorrow would be universal.

Cited in Ibn Abi Usaybia, *Uyun al-Anba fi tabaqat al-Atibba*; or
Important Information Concerning the Generations of Physicians (AD 1242).
Based in part on the translation in Paul and Lesley Murdin, *Supernovae*
(Cambridge: Cambridge University Press, 1985).

THIS YEAR ALL THE MIRRORS HAVE SHATTERED

For Helen

and the mansion is a labyrinth of reflections,
corridors shards, rooms fragments, faces cubist.
Passageways lead to themselves. Kitchens
teem with the poor chewing cutlery.
In living rooms pianos have been detuned.
The library's shelves are full of hollow books
that double as ash-trays. Few speak aloud
though refined voices murmur through walls,
locked doors. You can hear the clink of bone
china, shuffling papers, a gavel. In the cellar
there is sobbing, clanking of chains,
the smell of burning. No-one ventures down
to see what's there. Somewhere in the maze
is a lost self holding a loved one's hand
but you'll never find your way back again.
On coffee tables are newspapers full of lies
about an outside world clamouring to get in—
as if anyone would want to come here,
as if anything exists beyond the front door.

CRAP ALLEGORY

For Stuart

We need to talk about the burnt-out tower
a fuck-off middle finger
raised to gentrification
in a rich part of London.

We should speak about the burnt-out tower
an immigrants' incinerator
blackened by poverty
against a bourgeois sky.

I want to write about the burnt-out tower
how ash rained down in showers
onto white BMWs.
Drivers had to put wipers on full.

I want to but I can't write about this—
it's a crap symbol, far too obvious,
a modern Gormenghast made unambiguous
or some crude medieval allegory
starring the Desperate and the Greedy.
Reality like politics makes for shit poetry
which cannot contain the smoke the smoke the smoke the
smoke the smoke the smoke the smoke the smoke the smoke
the smoke the smoke the smoke the smoke the smoke the
smoke the smoke the smoke the smoke the smoke the smoke
the smoke the smoke the smoke the smoke the smoke the
smoke the smoke the smoke the smoke the smoke the

OEDIPUS AND TIRESIAS

After Sophocles

Beloved Oedipus,
there will always be a Tiresias
sitting tight-lipped in the corner
of chamber, pub or courtroom,
not saying what he is thinking,
his eyeballs an opaque mirror
on plague, famine, massacre,
a city of wailing and ashes.

Beloved Oedipus,
you can interrogate him,
beat him, even arrest him
for silence under oath,
deviancy, transgenderism
or for your father's murder
(as you have many others)
but still you see what he sees
within and cannot unsee it
despite dossiers, ministers,
secret police and newspapers.

Beloved Oedipus,
you can kill him as your father
or fuck him as your mother
or both. It hardly matters
for there'll always be others
somewhere in the crowd
blindly knowing what you
have done in the past
and will continue to do.

Or maybe one day,
beloved Oedipus,
you'll even take his place,
donning sackcloth and ashes,
haunting foreign cities,
eye sockets bleeding truth,
leaving a trail like history.

FROM THE PROPHECY OF NEFERTI,
c.1991–1786 BCE

You know not what you ask,
most reverend Majesty,
when you tax me, Neferti,
to tell you not of the past
or present but of the future.

Your Majesty, I cannot
and will not lie to you
about that time of calamity
when the Nile will run dry
while its banks are flooded,
when winds of the four quarters
will fight with one another,
when alien birds will breed
in the swamps of the Delta
devouring all the fish there
so the fishermen starve.

In that unending twilight
when great Re is veiled
and none can sleep,
servants will become masters,
brothers will fight brothers,
sons will murder fathers
with arrows of strange metals,
husbands will turn away
while wives are raped,
all will laugh at others'
pain, suffering, death
and no-one will dress hair
as is the custom for funerals.

Instead, the living will abide
in the necropolis while corpses
remain unburied, unmourned,
floating downstream to the sea.
Only then will they know peace,
freed from the horrors of futurity,
the source of all our miseries.

After the translations by André Dollinger, Miriam Lichtheim and
R. B. Parkinson.

SUPERNOVA AD 185

For Will Buckingham

This guest star in the Southern Gate Constellation
was the size of a bamboo mat, five-hued,
eliciting delight and fury in equal measure.
It appeared during the tenth month of the second year
of the Zhongping era—being the sixtieth year
of the astrological cycle. Its brightness diminished
over the next few months and after six months vanished.
All astronomers knew the light foretold a terrible disaster
which duly took place in Luoyang, four years later.
Yuan Shao, the respected Metropolitan Commandant,
murdered two thousand officials and eunuchs.
Then General in Chief Wu Kuang and his army
attacked and defeated the armies of He Miao
who was General of Chariots and Cavalry
and the dead numbered many thousands of men.
Thus we are encircled by a million stars, permanent
and guest, each and every one of them
if read rightly foretelling a massacre to come.

Based on a translation by Will Buckingham of *The Book of the Later Han*, c.445 AD (Astronomy, Latter Section).

THE PESSIMIST'S HOROSCOPE

This month Saturn and Jupiter are in conjunction
so if you set yourself goals you won't achieve them.

Be honest and assertive in your professional life
and Neptune and your bosses will shaft you anyway.

The Moon is shadowing unpredictable Uranus
so watch out for bankruptcy on Monday.

Keep hold of your worries: with ascendant Mercury
your ticket stands no chance of winning the lottery.

Single? Venus is sinking in your chart
so romance will probably flip you the bird.

Attached? The evening star will ensure
you won't be for much longer

and with your constellation below the horizon
you will cry
and cry
and cry

CASSANDRA COMPLEX, 2003

After Aeschylus

Agamemnon, do not go into that house.

Do not go into that house where the very walls
bleed, the windows weep for past and future,
where even Gods dare not linger.

Do not go into that house of slaughter,
where fathers sleep with daughters
and sons are dismembered, eaten.

Believe me, believe me, Agamemnon,
do not enter there where a monster
lurks beneath the mask of Clytemnestra.

I know you will not listen to me, Agamemnon,
because of the curse Apollo spat in my mouth.
It is not you nor myself I care about.

There is nothing I have not suffered already
in Troy and you deserve what happens today
for what you did to your daughter at Aulis.

What will happen today is your fault
as it is your wife's and that of Aegisthus,
offspring of ungodly incest.

This house was built on your family's sins
but if you go in so too will our twins
and all our children's children

will be sucked into this terrible vortex
where blood will drip from walls
dark as oil for generations to come.

Turn back before it is too late, Agamemnon.
Or maybe after all Achilles was right
and you really are a fucking idiot.

MAY 2008

For R.

Born premature, as if in the red,
we dreamt you a compensatory future
in the black, your incubator
a mini-limousine chauffeuring
you away from broke Leicester,
hapless father, ill mother,
softer twin who preferred sleep to shares,
your eyes white open with dollar signs,
a sleep-suited Sugar,
a scratch-mitted JR,
with only two pounds to your name.

2nd MVT

.

CHIROMANCY

After Heinrich Cornelius Agrippa von Nettesheim, *De incertitudine et vanitate scientiarum* (1527), and *De occulta philosophia* (1531–3).

Of the fundamental importance of similitude
I have spoken elsewhere: the palm's landscape
is a Little World of mountains, valleys, riverbeds
like that of Earth and each of its seven elevations
represents one of the seven heavenly bodies
which sing to the others according to the intervals
of music, intervals which are, in turn, played out
in the proportions of the hand's finger joints.
As the Ancients knew, so too in modern times
do many of our finest physicians, Peter of Appo,
Albert the Teutonic, Antiochus Bartholemeus,
Michael Scotus, Coclitis and Andreas Corvus,
all is thus in harmony and as long as God sees fit
to maintain the same number of peaks on a palm
and the same number of planets in the sky
to read a palm is to see in it the stars' reflection
and to hearken to the celestial musical harmonies
which bind all worlds, large and small, into one.

DETERMINISM

On the occasion of a tenth anniversary

Because I wasn't yet too drunk to see your legs
(because the Union watered down its pints),
because you'd got over tonsillitis
and wanted to see some band I can't recall,
because that morning your crisps were heart-shaped,
because you'd gone to Warwick not thank God Oxford,
because (slow as ever) I'd taken too long to do my course,
because you'd wanted to escape a home
of arranged marriages, forced exile, angry relatives,

and no doubt (therefore) because of previous marriages,
forced exile, angry relatives,
so because of '74, invasions, displacements,
and on my family's side because of 1930s poverty,
people marrying people they shouldn't,
children and money changing hands,
and later because of divorce, ECT, second marriages,

all with roots in post-World War I depression,
World War I itself, what happened to an Archduke,
industrial revolutions in Britain and Germany,
(particularly that of the cotton industry),
and ultimately because of pre-industrial feudalism,
in Britain or Cyprus or somewhere else,
as well as apes, evolution, language, tools,
that bloody butterfly who's always flapping his wings in Rio
causing hurricanes in Moscow
even before Rio and Moscow were invented—
and, long before butterflies, Rio or Russia,
a fourteen-billion-year-long pre-history back to a first because,

and because, if space-time isn't linear, somewhere in the future
dreaming of being born were Rosie and Miranda,

because of everything
(which is, no doubt, philosophically speaking,
the same as saying nothing),
I asked you if you wanted a drink
and you said yes
and—without sounding overly bathetic about it—
a universe was in those words.

HOW TO DO BEST WHATEVER IT IS YOU ARE DOING

Extracts from *Enuma Anu Enlil*

I.   Diviner's Manual

Remember there are twelve months in the year
and 360 days. If you know the year's length
and read these tablets for the meanings
of appearances and disappearances of Iku
and other stars, the position of the sun
and moon in the months of Addaru and Ululu,
the risings of the Pleiades and how such signs
of the sky combine with those of the earth,
then you will understand what such signs meant
before and hence what they will mean again.
If you look up an evil portent and find the timing
confirmed you cannot pass it by and the illness,
famine or death will most certainly take place
unless you can find a sign to counteract the first.
To know the signs of earth and sky in this way
will help you do best whatever it is you are doing.

II. From Omens of Sunrise

If the sunrise is speckled with blood and the light is cool
in the month of Nisannu rebellions will be constant
and Adad the Storm God will devour all.

If on the first day of Nisannu the sunrise is splattered
with blood grain will not grow, there will be famine
and the starved will eat human flesh.

If on the first day of Nisannu the sunrise is splattered
with blood and the light is cool the king will die and
mourning will not cease in the land.

III. From Omens of Venus

If Venus's disk is dark and its light dirty
the king will be merciless
and imprison his own people.

If Venus's disk is present with two others
on either side the king will treat his people well
but still the city walls will fall and the people disperse.

If on the first of Nisannu two disks appear
the king will die.

If on the eleventh of Nisannu three disks appear
a whole army will die.

IV. From *Shumma Alu*: Everyday Omens

If the outside of the house is decorative
it will be deserted.

If the outside of the house is beautiful
it will not stand long.

If the house keeps changing outside
so will its keepers inside.

If the house is ugly or in shade
all inside will be happy.

If the house's exterior looks ordinary
its keepers will grow old together.

From *When the Gods Anu and Enlil* ... Based on translations in A. Leo
Oppenheim, 'A Babylonian Diviner's Manual,' *Journal of Near Eastern Studies*,
33:2 (1974), 197–220, the British Museum, and www.mesopotamia.co.uk.

HIPPARCHIA OF MARONEIA'S FINAL LETTER TO CRATES OF THEBES, c.300 BCE

I know, my beloved Crates, that time will destroy my thoughts
and writings, casting them to the four winds like so much trash
just as Theodorus tore away my double cloak at Lysimachus's party
that long-ago day when you and I were first married. Remember?
He scolded me and asked me, quoting Euripides, if I was that harridan
who had abandoned loom, duty, housework? And I stood up to him
naked in front of the whole male assembly—just as, after I am dead,
I will stand up to time itself—and told him yes, I was that woman
but I would never regret leaving behind the back-ache of weaving,
high-heeled shoes, fashionable robes held together with brooches,
in favour of a staff, a satchel, sex in porticos with you, my beloved,
and a philosophy which will survive me in practice if not in words.

A PYROMANCER'S ADVICE TO HER DAUGHTER, SHANG DYNASTY, c.1200 BCE

Daughter, first scrub the bone free of ox-meat and blood
for any trace of these substances will seem to offend
the ancestors who being royal have delicate constitutions.
You can polish the bone too if you want to impress.

Next use the drill to make the requisite holes pretending
the pattern is random. Carve the date and your name
into the oracle bone. Inscribe the King's name if you must
followed by the charge He wants put to his ancestors:

will the floods come tomorrow or not? Will He have a son
or not? Is it likely there will be an earthquake or invasion?
Are 1,000 sacrifices sufficient for this year's harvest?
Is His toothache caused by an angry ancestor or aunt?

Afterward, apply the orange poker to the drilled holes
as I have shown you and observe how the bone cracks.
The cracks will point towards one or other of the answers
depending on how you fixed the holes beforehand.

Do not listen to the other diviners: the secret is not to flatter
but rather to conjure in the King's mind doubt and terror
and hence bind Him to your dragon future with pessimism
to the point that He won't dare take a piss without asking.

Oracle bones, also known as dragon bones, were pieces of turtle shell,
ox scapulae, or suchlike used for divination by fire (pyromancy) in
ancient China, c.1500–1000 BCE.

PAGLIACCI

For Kershia

> The same scourge whips the joker and the enjoyer of the joke.
> – Ralph Waldo Emerson, 'The Comic'

Take my advice, said the Parisian doctor:
mix in different circles, try Italian theatre.
This all-consuming melancholy, sir,
it's a mere spectre of your imagination.

Swallow these pills by all means, sir,
but you also need to get out and about.
You're in Naples. Make the most of it,
seek out pleasurable society.

Go and see the great clown Carlini—
I hear he has the whole city in fits.
If your gloom can withstand his antics,
it must be incurable indeed.

He's sure to take you out of yourself,
sir, give life a humorous complexion,
help you to pull up your stockings
as I think they say back in England.

Carlini: he's your panacea, my friend.
He will make you laugh till you cry.
His jokes, they will split your sides
(again as the English sometimes say).

But it's no good, the patient said back:
I already attend the Italian theatre nightly
because I am myself that great Carlini
and can hardly make myself laugh
except perhaps at my own misery.

Based on a story recounted by Ralph Waldo Emerson, F. Wiseman,
Charles Dickens, George Mikes and others.

CALIGULA'S WAR AT SEA

After Gaius Suetonius Tranquillus and Robert Graves

Of course we had to declare war on the sea:
Neptune, that Greek, is Jove's—which is to say our—
oldest enemy and we knew he might attack
the Empire in minutes, launching his spring tides,
his wrecking storms, his waves of mass destruction.
Our only option was pre-emptive retaliation—
the centurions, even legionaries knew that.
None questioned us. And any we saw half-heartedly
chopping sand, skewering surf, paddling ankle-deep
were staked to gull-infested cliffs so Neptune's air-force
might peck out their eyes.

What booty we took from him! Chests of seashells,
pebbles smashed in battle, fish writhing
like prisoners of war. We captured four fishermen
in league with him to burn in cages back home.
Finally he sued for an ignominious peace.
We commissioned a lighthouse to be built
to keep watch and betook our spoils to Rome
where our armies were feted as conquering heroes.
Everyone knew we had to do it.
Everyone understood.

Only those damned shells seem to mock me:
however many I smash, when I put one to my ear
all I can hear is the sea, laughing.

LAUGHTER EPIDEMIC

It all started with besuited newsreaders
sniggering while reporting a massacre:
anchors passed it on to correspondents
who passed it on to interviewees
who infected millions of viewers.

A neurologist compared it to the plague
in Tanganyika, '62, but was crying before
he could finish. His po-faced colleague
diagnosed mass psychogenic illness
but farted before she'd concluded too,
as if hysteria had to escape somehow.

No-one could stop themselves:
the Chancellor couldn't take his cuts
seriously; the PM declared war
as if inviting everyone to a party;
brass bands snorted at the cenotaph,
historians and students at history;
Alzheimer's and cancer were side-splitting
for untreated patients and their families.
Refugees turned back, scared of contagion.

Parliament dissolved for the election
in fits of posh giggles. There were reports
of voters dying, their hearts exhausted
by comic speeches, promises like jokes,
an outbreak of national hilarity
as unending as despair.

ELECTION NIGHT 2015

A pink-spotted giraffe is breaking the News
to mumbled gasps from stuffed voters
that the Crocodile Party has been swept from power
in favour of a new coalition government
of the Cat and Middle-Sized Bear Parties.

There'll be a lot of political manoeuvring
in the coming minutes, maybe even tickling,
but the two parties at least share a policy platform
of: 1. making everyone's dreams come true
and 2. compulsory bed-bouncing.

The crocodiles have declined to comment
but rumour has it they may be contemplating
a last-ditch *coup d'état*
by gobbling up all their enemies.

ELECTION POST-MORTEM

Following the election pundits explained
why the pundits had got it so wrong.

We are sorry, they said.
We underestimated the People, they said,
their universal love for one another,
their beautiful way with strangers.

Our polls were black holes
sucking in the light.
Our pie-charts were sieves
through which a hidden wellspring
of crypto-hippies tumbled.
We didn't film our nation's march
hand in hand toward the sunset.
Our cameras were pointed at the dark

so we mistook inner-city waltzes for riots,
bankers' hand-outs for looting,
ribbon-wrapped parcels for bombs
and poetry for politics.

It's easily done.

PITCH FOR A HORROR MOVIE

After Susan Sontag

We'll need a bunch of twenty-somethings
including two hunks, plus Hysterical Blonde
and Resourceful Redhead who'll look hot
when her top's slashed and torn.

They go SOMEWHERE camping—somewhere
cellphones don't work—woods, nature and shit.
They meet two hicks in dungarees who live
on the edge of said forest who warn them off.
Hysterical Blonde wants to go back home.
All she cares about, claims Redhead,
is her pedicurist and lipstick.

They set up camp and there's some sex—
we need it with nipples early on.
After, there's a row and Hysterical Blonde
runs off crying to be scared by SOMETHING
half seen in the trees: say, a grunting bloke
in a mask with limp and machete.
Back at camp no-one believes her.

Next day they get lost in the woods.
Lots of to-ing and fro-ing, a huge chase,
and they're all butchered in weird ways—
loads of gore—except Resourceful Redhead.
She seems to get away, but from behind
is surprised and knocked out.

She comes to in a cave hung with friends'
body parts. She escapes and is pursued
through the woods by Grunting Bloke —
he's much faster than her despite the limp.
Her clothes are torn and her boobs covered
in mud and blood and sweat.

Finally she reaches the hicks' house.
They welcome her but then the BIG TWIST:
turns out they're in on it too. Grunting Bloke
appears and they hold her down together.

Or BIGGER TWIST: actually, *she*'s in on it
and it's all been an act to get rid of her friends
so she can settle down with Grunting Bloke.

Or even BIGGER TWIST: Hysterical Blonde
comes back from the dead to butcher everyone
except Resourceful Redhead with whom
she's been having a secret fling.
There's a final bloody lesbian snog
before black-out, end titles.

(Or FINAL TWIST: during the snog,
one of them stabs the other in the back.
FINAL-FINAL TWIST: we stab the audience
in the back. Or not. Or yes. Or not. Or yes.
Whatever you want. Who the fuck cares).

THE TALE OF THE KING AND THE GHOST

The beautiful ghost that appeared
before great King Neferkare
was neither from sky nor earth
but hovered somewhere between,
his tears ringing him like a halo.

The King was not frightened
but addressed the spirit directly:
"Welcome back to Memphis
in the name of Ptah, my son.
Why do you weep this way?"

The ghost-boy answered:
"Don't you know me, my Lord?
I am Khentyka's son Snefer.
I cry because in Osiris's realm
all that remains for me is the past,
while all you have is the future.
You can look to the rising sun
while I only ever see it setting.
We are forever sundered, Lord,
and however much I desire it
I can never again touch you."

Then the King shed a tear too
because he had loved Snefer,
Khentyka's boy, once. Hearing
of this grief, the necropolises
burst open and the Nile's banks
overflowed with the tears
of ghosts who could no longer
touch the future, their grief
outweighing that of the living
as ten thousand deben
to a single feather.

The flood only abated after
many of the dead were reunited
with brothers and lovers
drowned by Anuket and Sobek.
Neferkare was not among them
and Snefer, Khentyka's boy,
mournfully faded away
leaving his King to the future—
toward which the latter hurried
as if into the anaesthetizing
embrace of Ammit the Devourer.

From the Middle Kingdom, 2000–1700 BCE. Elaborated from the
fragment translated by R. B. Parkinson.

GOTHIC

Even the weather was in on the act,
shrouding Whitby Abbey in fog,
whipping up the sea into half-hearted
choppiness. The hotel was packed
with taxidermy, imbecilic mammals
grinning from every corner,
out-of-tune pianos which could
play themselves. Dracula Museum
broadcast doom to the harbour
and all the fish and chip shops.

We were there with our twins
(which should've been uncanny
but wasn't). In the two-penny
arcade a guy with a bleeding fist
threatened to punch me, seemed
for a moment the one genuine thing
in the place. But even he couldn't
be bothered in the end.

TOOTH

in intensive care after the op he bit
right through his lower mouth
so we could see the tooth through a hole
as if unable to speak the pain was trying
to find another way out
so they brought in a dentist one day
who extracted the offending tooth
and sewed up the hole
because pain unlike a soul
cannot get out
must not hover over a sickbed
head toward the light
speak a comprehensible language
paint *The Scream*
beat a percussion instrument loudly
even just cry

A CHAOS THEORY OF PARKINSON'S

After Oliver Sacks, *Awakenings*

A butterfly flutter in one finger
might spiral into a storm of tremors.

Microclimates of shaking paralyses
might coalesce into a snowflake waltz.

L-Dopa minutely under the ideal dose
might cause a lightning-strike fall.

And you never know such a fall
might unlock a long-caged memory

like a rainbow of butterflies
released into sky.

AWAKENINGS

After Oliver Sacks

For nurses the postencephalitics seemed petrified
their personalities paralytically im-prism-ed.
L-Dopa was a beam of light shot through them
refracted, split, rainbowed, bent, shattered.

SHOSTAKOVICH, STRING QUARTET NO.11

notes are misfiring neurons
in a quartet's nervous system

glissandi like Tourette's
shitfuckbollocksharmonics
dissonances like seizures
seizures epileptic dissonances
in the cello's temporal lobe
fuckshitbollocksharmonics
fugues and canons started then forgotten
what was I saying again?
poliomyelitic paralysis superimposed on mania superimposed on
poliomyelitic paralysis superimposed on maniaonmaniaonmania on

heart attack   stroke

after death second violin twitching between two notes
a corpse convulsing
E and G E and G E and G E and G E and G E G E G E G E

his funeral march Parkinsonian
full of fits   starts   jerks   shuffles   staggers   falls

falls

falls

till all that remains are dreams of past illnesses
as if dementia not the soul survives death
a long-held high C on a violin that never

SHOSTAKOVICH, STRING QUARTET NO.15

Play it so that flies drop dead in mid-air.
— Dmitri Shostakovich, 1974

The quartet is a pesticide
purging concert halls
of counter-revolutionary insects.

It deports them to a Gulag of adagios
a sonata confinement
beyond the Arctic Circle of harmony
where only B-flat screeches
echo through bars, prison walls
ppp ——————— *sffff*
tortured buzzes like violins.

Sometimes they re-attempt flight
in solo cadenzas
even half-remembered waltzes
but this funeral march is entomological
and will tear their wings
from their abdomens.

Afterward you can hear tiny families
rubbing legs together for warmth.
Above a mantelpiece is a photo
with a fly-shaped hole. Memories,
drones, cries fade *morendo morendo.*

3rd MVT

SIBELIUS LETZTEN GEDANKEN

> Widespread they stand, the Northland's dusky forests,
> Ancient, mysterious, brooding savage dreams;
> Within them dwells the Forest's mighty God,
> And wood-sprites in the gloom weave magic secrets.
> – Jean Sibelius, *Tapiola*

... and for decades after 1926
and your Opus 112
that was you, wasn't it?,
weaving your magic secrets
with wood-encased graphite
on wood pulp for a forest
of bows and gut

    and ultimately
with the burning wood of '45
when your Eighth Secret
which had tantalised
conductors, listeners, visitors
to Ainola and Kammiokatu—
Koussevitsky, Cameron, Paavola—
went up with diaries, letters,
the whole of Europe,

that great musical deforestation
leaving only a 1933 bill
to copy a silent first movement,

and the wood-sprites retreated
with their secret and savage dreams
to what remained of the wooded glooms,
their eyesight cataracted
by too-long exposure
to fire-light.

THE FALL OF THE CORAL TREE PEOPLE

From Popol Vuh, Sacred Book of the Quiché Maya People

These wooden effigies were weighed in the balance
and deemed a failed species for they could not
remember or worship or bleed or smile or cry.
So a great *Butic* was planned by the Heart of the Sky
and rain thick as sap poured down on their heads
and black waves surged around their bodies.

Afterward came the Chisellers of Faces
who gouged out their eyes and the Knives of Death
who cut off their heads and the Earth God sent Jaguars
who ambushed them and crunched their bones.
Their pets accused them of negligence and beatings
so abandoned them. Their turkeys and livestock
said they had eaten them so would in turn
feed on their flesh. Their grinding stones
said they were ground upon day and night
so would in turn grind the people like maize.
Then their tools nailed and sawed and drilled them
and their pots and pans roasted them on the fire.

Finally the disfigured remains of the effigies
fled in terror from the fire and tried to escape
to the rooftops but their houses sank beneath them.
They hid in caves but the cavemouths shut on them.
They climbed trees but the trees would not support them,
would not forgive them. Thus the whole world cursed them
and scattered them and turned their descendants into *K'oy*
to roam the mountains and serve as warnings to the future
and to all species who came after.

Inspired by the translation by Allen J. Christenson, 2007.
Butic: flood
K'oy: spider-monkeys

MUSICAL ANTHROPOCENE

After Thea Musgrave, *Green*, and Robert Macfarlane

We are the irruption of noise into music:
ariosos disintegrate in our hands
while discordant clusters round low F
shake the earth beneath our feet.

Our symphonic scores rot,
violins are resurrected as trees,
but that *tremolo* F remains below all
and remains to the last,
persistent as fossilised plastic
or a nuclear legacy radioactive
for 10,000 years.

Green is a short piece for twelve strings by Thea Musgrave,
commissioned by the Scottish Ensemble, and first performed in 2008.

THE INCREDULITY OF THOMAS

For Scott Freer

So first I touched that gap in his side
pierced by the spear. He didn't flinch,
but smiled at me, egged me on,
offering one hand and then the other,
guiding me to those nail-wounds,
letting my trembling fingers linger there,
holding my wrist while I stroked him.
I couldn't stop touching, touching,
circling those beautiful holes softened
by resurrection as if everlasting life
itself was crushed into that moment.
For I knew it was true: he was risen
from the dead and I adored him
with all my heart and finger-tips.
And I felt certain he loved me too—
after all, he seemed to enjoy my touch—
though he couldn't speak it out loud
in case his father heard.

EMIL NOLDE, *THE PROPHET* (1912)

He has gouged the future out of wood,
crucified his own face—
brow and nose a cross, eyes nails,
beard a modern Golgotha.

He cannot say: *Father, forgive them,*
for they know not what they do,
because his mouth is carved shut,
chiselled by himself into silence.

He has no wish to hear
what his self-portrait has to say
and cannot bear to know
what he sees beyond the frame.

THOMAS MÜNTZER ADDRESSES THE ETERNAL LEAGUE OF GOD, PRIOR TO THEIR DEFEAT AT THE BATTLE OF FRANKENHAUSEN, 15 MAY 1525

For John Lucas

Fuck that over-fed pig Luther and his godless princes.
Fear God, not these rotten fruit who have never known pain
nor the cutting edge of the ploughshare and hence can
never know heaven. We have been sent to harvest them.

It's true, a hundred thousand brothers are already dead
but better to die together than be martyrs for Satan.
The End of Days is upon us and we can never be saved
if we stand alone. Our salvation can only be collective.

It doesn't matter that many of you cannot read the Bible.
There are thousands who can who will still combust in hell
while we stand together, laughing. Faith doesn't lie in
signs on a page but in your suffering, Christ's crucifixion,

the pain of which exceeds all writing and which we alone,
my peasant-brothers, share. I preached this in Zwickau,
Allstedt and Mühlhausen and this is what I need you
to remember now. Look to the sky above Frankenhausen:

our Lord has sent a rainbow to show He stands with us,
to show us we must no longer serve two masters on earth.
We must throw off our worldly shackles. Victory will be ours,
the birds of the sky will drink the rich man's blood, Luther
will be devoured by beasts, and God's Word will reign forever.
Brothers, it is rainbow-prophesied: *Omnia sunt communia*—
by the end of today, everything shall be held in common
and all will be well with us forever and ever. Amen.

JOSEPH GLANVILL RENOUNCES ASTROLOGY

> We need not be appalled by Blazing Stars, and a Comet is no
> more ground for Astrological presages than a flaming chimney.
> – Joseph Glanvill, *The Vanity of Dogmatizing*, 1661

I see now, in light of the peculiar discoveries of Brahe and others,
that the celestial bodies can foretell only themselves;
and in my dying dreams I look on a world forested with chimneys
where the firmament is filled with Blazing Stars and Comets
made by man of terrestrial matter. And I wish I might live
the thousand or so years it will take for this to come to pass
because then the present will surely be glorious and there will be
no need for fear, prediction or, indeed, the future.

THE GREAT INUNDATION

After a vision of Fr. Balthassar Mas, 1630

I dreamed of a great inundation, everything swallowed
by a wave moving up the Thames like a leviathan
until only England's highest turrets and steeples
reached above the flood. The best were saved,
lords and ladies on their battlements, clergymen
clinging to spires, hems of cassocks pulled away
from the drowning and the drowned.

Finally God sent a rainbow as the waters receded
a little. Those left were relieved and arranged
causeways of the heaped-up dead to France
or were rescued by strange flying contraptions
which swept down like angels and took them
to the fertile lands round the Nile and Red Sea
where they were greeted by many thousands
and went on to found new and better Englands.

MY IMAGINED COMMUNITY

is an earworm,
a half-recalled fragment
of a foreign folk-song.

Or it's something glimpsed
by a lone cyclist
in Malvern mists
(or deserted carpark,
or derelict Satanic mill),
never in full daylight,
never in chanting crowds

because its language comes alive
only on the lips of others
who talk in foreign cafés
of an illusion that is most itself
when not itself.

It is never found in tabloids
except in their apologies,
tiny columns on page 17
saying sorry like war poetry
for the battlefield of the past.

It breathes only in recollection,
only in Wordsworthian hindsight,
a memory of something
that was always (being) lost.

After Benedict Anderson, *Imagined Communities*, Edward Elgar,
Introduction and Allegro, and George Orwell, *The Lion and the Unicorn*.

ENIGMA

For H.W.

It is true that I have sketched for their amusement and mine the
idiosyncrasies of fourteen of my friends ... The Enigma I will not
explain—its 'dark saying' must be left unguessed ... Through and
over the whole set [of variations] another and larger theme 'goes,'
but is not played.
– Edward Elgar, 1899

The letter in which he said this is lost
and the fourteen friends are all dead
so they can't tell us what it meant
even if they knew in the first place.

There remain only the ghost-hunters
tracing spectral counterpoints
which weave in and out of variations,
walk through walls: counterpoints
like *Auld Lang Syne*, the *Dies Irae*,
Farewell and Adieu to You,
My Fair Spanish Ladies,
and Elgar's own *Black Knight*
with its identical intervals: pairs
of falling thirds divided by rising
fourth as the chorus sings
"He beholds his children die"—

as if shared by all true friendships,
weaving in and out of variations,
is an unheard Elgarian unconscious,
an enigmatic farewell and adieu,
a dark saying of grief.

NO DOUBT

No doubt I should present to you, discerning reader, an image,
something concrete, poignantly small like a rusting trowel—
though not that because he didn't like gardening—
an image through which you glimpse emotional truth.

No doubt there should be birds or butterflies flapping away
toward the horizon, and rain or a cruel sun laughing at me.
There should probably be an attic full of some hobby—
cobwebbed model trains giving rides to spiders
circling round and round in his absence—
but he didn't have a hobby, really, apart from TV sitcoms
which are inappropriately funny to mention in this context.

No doubt what I shouldn't do is tell you straight
that I loved him, miss him, close my eyes and dream him back
for you to class this poem unsentimental, English and good.

But to be frank these lines don't care what you or I think
and stubbornly refuse to be unsentimental, English, or good –
and, for that matter, they probably aren't even a poem.

THIS POEM IS TOO NEAT

The end of this poem will be too neat, too pat.
It will do that circular thing of coming back
to an image or memory at the start, of connecting
something very early with something sad
years later.

        The start of the poem will describe
my very first memory of leaving the outdoor
Art Deco lido in Trentham Gardens
which was full of dozens of mummies' bare legs
and was apparently closed when I was four.
I recall all of us shivering in towels in the car
and asking my father what pneumonia was
because he'd told us he'd get it if we didn't
leave right away. He explained what it was
and many years later he did get it and died.

I told you the end of this poem would be too neat,
too pat, as if a poem can lock you into a pattern
and there's no getting out of it.

REDUPLICATIVE PARAMNESIA,
SHREWSBURY FLOWER SHOW, 1997

For my father

During those two hours of panic we should have known
we'd find him not dawdling over decking or azaleas
but in the car park, patting for keys, trying to get home.

Even before right hemisphere malfunction
everything outside his front door seemed mere detour
every excursion an annoying prelude to recursion,

holidays just delays, work a hanging-on the bell for lunch, tea;
at concerts his palms pushed down on chair arms
prepared for triumphal return of the home key.

But now, whether in misrecognised living room, concert, work,
or on family day out in Shropshire, he's permanently lost,
inside or out, his whole world a reduplicating car park.

MY FATHER'S PARANOIA

That hot Sunday
he wanted the hedge cut very badly:
It must be done now, he said.
I said I'd do it when I was less busy
but that was too late for his paranoia
which was already muttering to him
that the *Evening Sentinel* would report him
for an overgrown hedge:
"Local Ex-Teacher's Hedge A Disgrace."
He reckoned the neighbours would spy on us
less easily with a trimmed hedge
(don't ask me how).

So he went out with secateurs, shears
and hacked at laurel and fir
as if they were the neighbours
and we couldn't stop him
even when he was in a sweat, trembling,
falling over, fitting, minor-stroking
on the ground, back in his chair,
his hands still jerkily pruning:
clip-clip-clip-clippety-clip,
paranoia still on his lips:
mustcutthehedgemustcutthehedge-
don'twanttheneighbourstoseethrough-
don'twantthepaperstoknow

and all I know now
is how un-busy I actually was
that hot Sunday.

KNOCKED OVER

For H.

My friends were disappointed it was only a yellow mini:
you could have chosen a Rover at least and a better colour.
They ate the Roses they brought for me next day themselves
doubly disappointed by my bruises, lack of broken bones.
It was different for my sister. When it happened the phone
started ringing back home and before my father picked it up
she was in tears and couldn't explain why. This was when
we were in our teens, not always together as we had been,
as if telepathy is a sign of a closeness already in the past.

UNDELIVERED LETTER FROM THE REV. CHARLES SMALE TO *THE TIMES*, 1874

Sir—

We have spent too long debating Mr. Darwin in these pages
whose theories, after all, are not incompatible with God
and His ever-unfolding map of history and future,
while that Bulldog, Prof. Huxley, has made grander claims
for Science and, as Carlyle might put it, the Steam Engine
Model of the World. Most recent is his pernicious
suggestion that consciousness is mere epiphenomenon,
no more than the 'steam-whistle which accompanies
the work of a locomotive engine with no influence
upon its machinery.'

         This, Sir, cuts to our very souls,
indeed to the Divine Mind which marshals those souls
toward a greater good: as if neither ourselves
nor our Lord can wield freewill, act on worldly matter,
direct our brute bodies to choose virtue over sin.

A steam-whistle is mere noise signifying nothing,
sending its vapours backward while the machine
thunders relentlessly forward; but if our mental
processes are akin to this, how then has
humankind studied anything apart from History,
ever raised its gaze to the future in Prophecy?
How, if Huxley is right, have we invented steam engines,
built cathedrals, penned symphonies, planned an empire?
How indeed have I resolved to write and post this letter?

I eagerly anticipate the future and Prof. Huxley's answer.

The quotation is taken from Thomas Henry Huxley's essay 'On the
Hypothesis that Animals are Automata, and Its History' (1874).

4th MVT

SUPERNOVA AD 1006; OR, HOW TO GET AHEAD IN THE WORKPLACE

During the third year of the Ching-tê reign
a guest star appeared west of Ti in the Lupus
constellation, three times the size of Venus,
casting shadows even during daytime.
Emperor Ching-tê and the people of Kaifong
were afraid it was coloured blue, a *kuo-huang*
or ill-omen portending calamity, warfare, famine.
Returning from his journey to Ling-nan,
Chou K'o-ming, Director of the Bureau
for Astronomy, consulted the *T'ien-wên-lu*
and *Ching-chou-chan* and declared instead
that since the star was yellow in colour
and *huang-huang-jan* in light this sign
was a *Chou-po*, a joyful omen or *ching-hsing*,
blessing a glorious Emperor and his nation
with much-deserved prosperity. All were content
to believe him—and the star certainly
blessed Chou K'o-ming himself, for he was soon
promoted to Chief Librarian and official Escort
of the Crown Prince, in recognition of services
to astrology, prophecy and truth.

After the biography of Chou K'o-ming, AD 954–1017, as featured in
David H. Clark and F. Richard Stephenson, *The Historical Supernovae*
(Oxford: Pergamon Press, 1977), and Paul and Lesley Murdin,
Supernovae (Cambridge: Cambridge University Press, 1985).

PERSON SPECIFICATION

You will be a high achiever
who knows everyone else is not.

You will be the kind of person who leads
by accepting a new company Audi
on a morning you announce redundancies.

You should have wide experience
in eating previously healthy organisations
from within. In terms of qualifications
you will hold grade A in Asset Stripping
and Parasitism.

You will have the skills necessary to tie
in knots of regulations anyone who needs
tying up. Deep down, you will believe
people rather like it. Leadership is bondage.
Remember, it's all about those acronyms:
BDSM—Bondage, Domination, Sado-
Managementism.

You will enjoy making jokes about bondage
to your personal assistant, as well as
relevant sexist or racist or ageist
(delete as appropriate) comments
and will be an expert at clarifying afterward
that any offence was the employee's fault
for not having a sense of humour.
After all, tone is everything for a leader
when faced with a tribunal.

You will like suits, football and golf
and you will have a family incarcerated
in a frame on your desk.

You will be happy to make *difficult decisions*
while dressing them up in frilly tutus.
Your cross-dressing decisions will curtsey,
pirouette, grand jeté, plié faster and faster
so all the mesmerised audience can do
is gasp and applaud and then file
out of the auditorium in an orderly fashion,
switching the lights off as they go.

SAVILE ROW

The white men in suits fucked up
the whole *Scooby Doo* ending
in an episode that'd lasted decades,
unmasking victims rather than culprit.
He'd never bothered wearing a mask
till he was buried. Afterward the suits
could be heard muttering remorsefully
into their swirling Chardonnay
We'd have gotten away with it too
if it wasn't for those grown-up kids
from retirement villas in Tuscany.

ERNST NEUSCHUL, *MESSIAS* (1919)

The Messiah will be a psychopath
crucifying you with his stare

giving you no choice but to follow
this starving Jew, this emaciated
Übermensch, whose rib-cage
is a prophecy. You will follow

him along a yellow-brick road
leading deep inside his self-

portrait until all that is left

of you

is I.

DAEDALUS AFTER KNOSSOS

The maze is now a seashell's
spiral threaded by an ant,
a miniature Ariadne
searching for honey,

as if sun-touching ambitions
are drowned in an ocean
and grief has compacted
Daedalian ingenuity
to an ever-diminishing point,

the minutiae of mourning
over three thousand years
reaching sub-atomic level,
a labyrinth of quantums
in which you are finally lost
and all of us are threadless.

Following the death of his son, Daedalus settled in Sicily. He was
discovered there by King Minos when he was asked to solve a riddle:
how to thread a spiral seashell. To do this, he tied a piece of string
round an ant, and lured the ant through the shell by placing honey at
the other end.

RONDO-BURLESKE

After Gustav Mahler, Symphony no.9 (1909)

Lost in a labyrinth of counterpoint
a polyphony of dead-ends
where Daedalian walls move
even the earth is no longer unironic
somewhere deep within
a minotaur's in a fugue
though he too is

lost in a labyrinth of counterpoint
a clew of tangled scales
marches leading nowhere
Léharian laughter in D minor
convulsive can-cans
and once a glimpse of sky
and song birds who aren't

lost in a labyrinth of counterpoint
but all exits are blocked
short-lived joy poisoned
hope deluded   vertigoed

by labyrinthine counterpoint
and somewhere deep within
the minotaur's roaring
rampaging through hedges
enraged by a redly-budding century
and the obscene tumescene of spring

GUSTAV MAHLER, SYMPHONY 10, 1910

Once written that nine-note discord—

a wound in A-flat minor
cut open by high A on trumpet—

can never be un-written
never be healed

never be exorcised
haunting everything after it

like the annunciation
of a wife's infidelity

like an orchestral unconscious
the dissonant repressed liberated
by a visit to Freud in Holland.

It lurks round the corner of every phrase
in the remainder of the *Adagio*

is lying in wait in the *Scherzo*s
is something to trip over in *Purgatorio*
is unleashed again in the finale

and even reminiscences
of long-ago *Adagiettos*
cannot stop it bleeding out of the score
into the twentieth century beyond.

MAHLER IN 1911

My life has all been paper.
— Gustav Mahler to Alma Mahler

I built godless cathedrals out of it,
upside-down Chinese pavilions,
sleigh-bell heavens, stained-glass hells,
tearing, folding orchestral sound like origami.

I shut my sick heart inside. For that I am sorry,
Alma. My very death will be a certificate,
a discord the Vienna Philharmonic can't play,
the *Entartete Musik* of a forgotten Jew.

And when the great conflagration comes,
as we know it must, a hundred million dots
will go up in smoke. Only ashes will remain,
falling back down like dissonance,

then settling like grey snow, like atonality.

ILSE WEBER

Her music seems to understand

that it is the simplest of C major progressions
which can show us the valley beyond the bridge,

that songs without medicine might soothe if not heal,
that only old-fashioned tonality might unlock
the gates of Theresienstadt,

that farewells are best phrased like blown kisses,
concise gestures from railway cattle-trucks,

that it is the womb-rocking of *Wiegenlieder*
returning us to long-forgotten sleep
which is most needed when children are praying
beneath pesticide showers.

Ilse Weber (1903–44) was a Jewish poet, children's writer,
broadcaster, producer and musician. Along with her husband and
second son, she was sent to Theresienstadt concentration camp in
1942, where she nursed sick Jewish children in the infirmary, and
continued writing songs and poems. Eventually, she was voluntarily
deported with many of her patients to Auschwitz, where she, her son
and the children were gassed on arrival.

XIUHMOLPILLI, OR THE BINDING OF THE YEARS, NOVEMBER 1507

After we'd thrown all our idols into the river,
broken up hearthstones, incense burners, furniture,
after the kitchens had been swept and our clothing burnt,
we fasted in darkness and awaited the end of the world.
At dusk the fire-priests, dressed as gods, left Tenochtitlan
silently along the southern causeway toward the temple
and the holy platform at the summit of Mount Huixachtlan.
There they watched to see if *Tianquiztli* would pass overhead
renewing time and our world for the next fifty-two years,
or if the demonesses would descend instead
to devour us all. Finally we witnessed the stars rise
and pass the meridian. As they travelled to the West
the priest of the Temple of Copulco took the *ixquauac*
and cut open the chosen boy's chest. In the cavity
he then kindled a fire with a wooden drill, pulled out
the burning heart and lit a beacon with it which we saw
from far below the Hill of Stars. Hence we knew
that the movements of the heavens had not ceased,
that our beloved Moctezuma's fears were unfounded,
that our city's fires would be relit and all would be well.

After Bernardino de Sahagún, *Florentine Codex: General History of the Things of New Spain*, Book 7, c.1585, ed. and trans. Arthur Anderson and Charles Dibble (Santa Fe: University of Utah Press, 2012).
Xiuhmolpilli: the Binding of the Years Ceremony, also known as the New Fire Ceremony
Tianquiztli: the Pleiades (literally, the Constellation of the Marketplace)
ixquauac: sacrificial flint knife

IANNIS XENAKIS, *PITHOPRAKTA* FOR TWO TROMBONES, STRINGS, XYLOPHONE AND WOODBLOCK (1955–6)

For Nouritza Matossian

the spontaneous architecture
of clouds
efflorescences
of *glissandi*

the probabilistic polyphony
of miniscule chaoses
within chaoses

col legno frappé
col legno frotté
arco bref   arco normal
rainbow of *pizzicati*

Brownian molecular motion
a cloudy palimpsest
beneath micro-wars of insects
and continent-wide armies

sometimes irregularly in-step
sometimes breaking
step on bridges
in case collective resonance
causes them to collapse

all is massing towards an entropic future
comprehended by no god except music
and a Maxwell-Boltzmann formula

After the description of *Pithoprakta* in Noritza Matossian, *Xenakis* (Nicosia: Moufflon, 2005).

ALFRED SCHNITTKE, SYMPHONY NO.5, CONCERTO GROSSO NO.4, 1988

> We have a different sense of time ... as a 'simultaneous chord.'
> – Alfred Schnittke

Spectres of Mahler
and no doubt Marx
are stalking the corridors
of a grand hotel in disrepair
round which Alfred is pedalling
never at rest
never at home.

Mahler's murmuring to himself
a ghostly piano quartet
he forgot to complete
(his memory's not what it was).

Marx props up the bar toasting his failures
or beckons seductively from the bath
his beard spread out
like a net.

Both Ms are decomposing.

Sometimes Alfred turns a corner
to be confronted by the pair
their voices a sudden shining:

Come and play with us, Alfred.
Come and play with us
forever and ever and ever and ever.

TITHONUS AND THE FIVE AGES OF THE UNIVERSE

Me only cruel immortality
Consumes: I wither slowly in thine arms,
Here at the quiet limit of the world,

fourteen billion years after the Primordial Era
only too aware that our swan-like Stelliferous Era
will after many a year dwindle toward its end
and all I have to look forward to
are the lights going out one by one
across the universe, galaxies coalescing,
stars burning down to embers,
till luminosity is but a memory.

Then will come the Degenerate Era
after a hundred or so trillion years
when the brand-newness of star-formation
is matter for photo-album-nostalgia
and there remain only brown dwarfs,
white dwarfs, all collapsing inward,
the universe spiralling down the drain

swallowed after 10 duodecillion years
by the Black Hole Era—
till even black holes evaporate

gradually bringing about
the unending end,
the Dark Era, 100^{100} years of waiting,
positrons, boredom and cold
in which particles pass one another
across the street, barely saying hello.

After that, well, there may be something else:
belated divine intervention, a crunch, a big rip
in which spacetime itself is torn to pieces

but I know I will still be here
remembering Ilion,
remembering you.

After Alfred Tennyson, 'Tithonus' (1860), and Fred Adams and
Gregory P. Laughlin, *The Five Ages of the Universe: Inside the Physics of the
Universe* (New York: Simon and Schuster, 1999).

TIME TRAVEL

Through an open door you're watching an old self
holding someone else's hand and you're trying to say:
Please don't let go. Please don't move away.
Please please please don't leave the room.

But something like the future is stuck in your throat
and the warning only comes out as a raven's croak
so the old self lets go, moves away, leaves the room,
walks through you as if it's you who's the ghost

as if it's you who'll be stuck here forever
with the someone else who stays in the chair
whose hand you're unable to touch
and who says confidently to the old you:
Goodbye, see you soon. See you very soon.